The Humbitious Woman®

HOW TO SELF PROMOTE IN THE WORKPLACE WITHOUT FEELING LIKE YOU'RE BRAGGING

JOCQUICE "JAE" SPIKES

THE HUMBITIOUS WOMAN®: HOW TO SELF PROMOTE IN THE WORKPLACE WITHOUT FEELING LIKE YOU'RE BRAGGING

Copyright © 2021 Jocquice Spikes

Printed in the United States of America.

ISBN 978-0-578-35259-6 (Paperback)

ISBN 978-1-0880-1686-2 (E-Book)

Published By: Jocquice Spikes Wisehat Consulting

Editor: I A.M. EDITING INK

Book Cover Design: I A.M. EDITING INK

Dedication

This book is dedicated to my husband, who has been my number one fan in all the ways that matter. Thank you for your understanding, support, and sacrifice. It reminds me of Ephesians 5:25 – "Husbands, love your wives, even as Christ also loved the church, and gave himself for it."

Thank you for giving yourself to me.

I love you.

Table of Contents

Preface

When I started my career nearly 24 years ago, I was undisciplined, un-coachable, and very insecure as a young woman of color. I had no plan, no guidance, and no one willing at that time to tell me the truth about my shortcomings. I nearly got fired for my chronic ability to show up to work late (did I mention that I was undisciplined?). This almost firing made me stop and realize that I had to do something. I knew that I was capable of more, but I found myself frustrated, burned out, and lacking the support I needed to accomplish my career goals. I had to figure out how to regain control of my career, overcome barriers, and establish true work/life harmony (because it will never be truly balanced, but we will get into that later).

One night, after praying for clarity and direction, I realized that ALL my issues began with me. I needed to change my **HAT** – my HABITS, ASSOCIATIONS, and THOUGHTS.

Once I changed my HAT, I completely changed my career and started seeing real opportunities and results. Changing my HAT allowed me to get two promotions and align with phenomenal mentors and leaders in the business. Over the years, I began helping others to succeed in their careers.

When you realize that everything you've ever gone through has been for your good and purpose in life, it changes your perspective. I founded WiseHAT® Consulting because I did not want to see another woman suffer in their career the way that I did. WiseHAT® Consulting empowers corporate women who feel stuck and burned out in their careers to change their HAT to take back control of their careers in order to excel and generate real opportunities.

As women, we wear so many hats: wife, mom, sister, friend, coworker, teacher, cleaner, organizer, business owner, I can go on and on. But none of them will be successful if you don't become a WiseHAT and apply wisdom to your Habits, Associations, and Thoughts. If you don't change your HAT in your career, it will directly impact how successful you'll be with all the other hats you're wearing.

This book is dedicated to the women who wear so many hats and still find themselves struggling with the overwhelming desire to be better than great yet lacking the boldness to state the facts of what they bring to the table in the workplace. It's time to get out of your own way! There's a reason why a football player doesn't try to play the game with a baseball hat on instead of a helmet. Likewise, a woman would not go to the Kentucky Derby with a Kangol hat on. The right hat establishes, prepares, supports, and sustains you. The right HAT (Habits, Associations, and Thoughts) will do the same. So, I say to you, ladies, it's time to change your HAT®!

Acknowledgments

Lord, I thank you for being a good Father. For being patient with me, for loving and understanding me like no one else can. Your word tells me to acknowledge you in all my ways, and you will direct my path. So, I acknowledge you in this book, and I thank you for planting the right people in my life at the right time to pour into me, mature me, mentor me, and push me. I see your love for me through these individuals, and it is amazing.

This book was born out of the many lessons I learned in my career. I'm grateful for those that took me under their wings and told me the truth about what it took to navigate my career successfully. I thank you all, and I am forever grateful for your mentorship.

PART ONE
True Humility

Birth of the Humbitious Woman

❧

"Know First Who You Are Then Adorn Yourself Accordingly"

— *EPICTETUS*

This quote might sound a bit cliché, but it is very true, especially the latter part. Many of us know exactly who we are; mighty powerhouses, capable of extraordinary greatness. The fact that we struggle to adorn ourselves accordingly when we know exactly who we are is illogical, so why do we struggle in this area?

For many of us, we were taught somewhere along the way to be humble and not talk about ourselves. But being humble does not mean you should be silent. Society's perception of humility will tell you that you can never own your greatness or take credit for the value that you bring. The proof of that can be found by simply looking up the antonym for humility in a thesaurus. You'll find words like boldness, confidence, and assertiveness. However, the true opposite of the word humility is arrogance and pride. Humility is not about thinking less of yourself but about thinking of yourself less; it is a true posture of servanthood.

Let's pause right here so I can clarify some things. As a leader, your responsibility is to make the job of those working with you, for you, and beside you easier. If you're not doing that, then you're not a leader. Leadership is a heavy word that gets thrown around a lot in Corporate America. Often people give themselves the title of leader. Still, they are not performing the word's true meaning (but that is another book for another time).

Now, back to my original point of humility in the workplace. True humility is about thinking of yourself less and is about serving others. Just because your focus is serving others, that does not mean that you should quietly go about serving without ever being able to talk about the impact that your servanthood has brought to the workplace. To do that would be operating in a false sense of humility. Say this with me out loud, "I **can** be humble and still be assertive, confident, and bold."

Over the years, I've had the pleasure of leading diverse teams comprised of both men and women, and every time their annual accomplishments were due, the women struggled so much with articulating the value they brought to the business that year. They would say to me, "Jae, I feel like I'm bragging." I found myself debating with them constantly over this, explaining that they are not bragging but simply stating facts. I would ask them, "Did you do it?" If the answer is "yes," then it is a fact, not a brag!

Know this, when the time comes to say how you contributed to your company, it is your job to remind them why they hired you (yes, they do need to be reminded). Saying nothing is not an option. Saying nothing is actually saying something- it's saying you either didn't bring any value or you don't care enough about your career to take the time to talk about the value you bring. Either way, the outcome won't be what you want. We must learn to be what I call a humbitious woman® - a woman who is both humble and ambitious.

humbitious
[hum-**bish**-*uhs*]

adjective
having humility **and** ambition; being confident in who you are, not
thinking less of yourself but thinking of yourself less, while also
being
desirous of achieving or obtaining success, having an earnest desire
for achievement or a specific goal that requires exceptional effort.

Early in my corporate career, I struggled with taking credit for the
things I accomplished and figuring out how to articulate the value I
brought to the business. When it was time to submit my accomplishments, I used to dread it. I was overwhelmed by the flood of
emotions, feeling frustrated, inadequate, and guilty about the entire
process. Frustrated because I did not feel like this was necessary.
Inadequate because it seemed everyone else had it all figured out,
and guilty because I did not know what to say, and I knew I should
know. I had often attributed these feelings to being my "authentic
self" because I was confident but not arrogant, and somehow, if I
took credit for my work, it would mean that I was embellishing.

As crazy as this sounds, it resonated with me so deeply that I often
ended up not saying much about the work I had done and how I'd
made huge strides, putting my blood, sweat, and tears into the business for that past year. As a result, my performance rating suffered,
which meant my salary suffered. This was followed by the vicious
cycle of me placing the blame on my leadership. I would tell myself,
"They saw how hard I worked; they knew everything that I'd done.
So why did I need to tell them what they already knew? Why
couldn't they just see it and award me accordingly?"

The truth is that there is no way that your leadership knows of
everything that you do; it is impossible. In fact, you should be
telling them the reason why they hired you, the reason why your
skills saved the company money or brought in additional revenue,

and it should be documented. If you owned the company, wouldn't you want to know the value each person brought to the table? Wouldn't you want to know how an employee saved you money or brought in additional revenue? The truth is that when you talk about these things, you are not bragging; you are stating facts. Stating facts about what you accomplished should not make you feel like you are bragging.

Compare this concept to a marriage. Once a couple gets married, does that mean they don't take the time to express their love for one another? Is the marriage ceremony the only time you'll ever express how valuable you are to one another? In the same way, the day that the company hired you should not be the only time you express the value you bring, nor should it be the only time the company expresses its gratitude for you.

Once I overcame this issue, I developed a passion for sharing the concepts that I'd developed to help me in this area, so I started hosting webinars at work about how to write effective accomplishments, and hundreds of women would show up. It seemed to only be a phenomenon that women dealt with. The men that I managed did not have this issue, so where did it come from? I was fortunate to have a great mentor that helped me overcome this issue, but I could not help but wonder why so many women struggled with the same thing. My pre-marital counseling sessions (another topic for another time) taught me that I needed to go back to my childhood to explore why this issue existed for me. It is my hope that my story and discovery will help you overcome as well.

Seen But Not Heard

PERMISSION TO RAISE YOUR HAND

"Children should be seen and not heard."

T hat was one of my parent's mottos. We were only allowed to speak when spoken to. Interrupting a "grown folks conversation" was equivalent to blasphemy. We had to obtain permission to speak. While I understand today as an adult that my parents were attempting to teach me good manners, I also realize that "good manners" will sometimes hold you hostage. As the saying goes, "a closed mouth will never get you fed."

Growing up, I had this competing narrative about when to speak up for myself, which carried through to my adulthood and career. I found myself sitting in board rooms and on conference calls, having everything to say and no way to say it. I would spend time in these meetings distracted by the conversation within, trying to convince myself to speak up. By the time I would get the courage to do so, the meeting would be over. I would say to myself, who are you to speak up? Was my idea that good anyway? Was it really going to bring value to the table?

What was happening? I felt that I needed permission to be heard – permission to raise my hand. I believed I was in a "grown folks conversation," and I had no right to speak. The truth is, I was brought to the table for a reason. My input was valued, or I would not have received the invite. I read somewhere that people cannot see your Thoughts, so how do they know what you think? By what they see you doing! And I was doing and saying nothing!

Unfortunately, this happens quite often to women for various reasons. Many women believe they should be seen and not heard. Some are even taught that it's God-ordained, and that couldn't be further from the truth. As a result, our voices are muffled, especially in the workplace. For years I walked around with this guilt and fear of thinking that if I spoke up for myself and expressed my thoughts, that somehow, I would be scolded for having the audacity to actually contribute in the workplace and to articulate what those contributions were. To say this was frustrating is an understatement. I had all these desires and ambitions. I saw myself operating in a much larger leadership role in my career, but I knew I could not get there if I could not speak up for myself.

Find Your Voice

NO PERMISSION REQUIRED

I still remember it like it was yesterday. I was in the process of getting my undergraduate degree while also working full time, and I had to submit my tuition reimbursement forms. I walked into my director's office to gain the signatures. He looked at the forms and asked me how I liked my job. I don't know what I was thinking, but I proceeded to tell him that the job was boring due to all of the automation, and I wanted a challenge. He smiled at me, signed the form, and I went back to work.

The next week, my supervisor and I were called into our regional manager's office with no reason given. My supervisor asked me on the way up the stairs, "Do you know what this is about"? I told her I had no clue, and I didn't. With every step, I was increasingly nervous. Once we made it into the office, our regional manager invited us to have a seat. At this point, I thought that I was about to be laid off, and my heart was pounding. When she proceeded to tell us that I was being temporarily promoted to handle a special project, and if it all worked out, my promotion would be permanent, I nearly fell out of my chair!

My manager and I were both in shock as we heard the additional details. I could not believe what I was hearing. Then I quickly thought about the conversation I'd had the week prior with my director, and it all made sense. I told him I wanted a challenge, and he handed me one! Once the fear and shock wore off and I got back to my desk, I sat there and reflected on what had just happened. Good manners would have required me to politely answer my director and say that I loved the job and everything was fine. I defied "good manners" and spoke my truth. I did not need anyone's permission. I had found my voice- albeit by accident, but I found it!

That promotion laid the foundation for the leader that I would become in the workplace. In one week, I went from a data entry role to managing a group of nine design and technical engineers. One might say that my director was crazy to do that. But I now know that he saw my potential to become a great leader, but I'm convinced that he may not have come to that conclusion so quickly if I'd not spoken up that day. My boredom quickly moved to an overwhelming sense of responsibility for my team being successful, and we were. The problem now was that I struggled to take credit for the hard work that we did.

When it came time for me to articulate our team's value to the organization, I clammed up. I begin to feel like if I actually documented these things and spoke about our herculean accomplishments, I would somehow be bragging. I did not want to be viewed as a bragger, despite being very proud of my team. In business, it's all about the data. As the saying goes, "you can't manage what you can't measure." If I could not take the time to truly show how my team was successful and clearly show the value we brought to the table, the fact that my director's choice to promote me provided a huge return on investment, then I was not going to make it very far.

My team had been responsible for clearing months of backlogged orders for business customers, which amounted to thousands of orders and millions of dollars in revenue. We partnered with many other internal and external teams, tracked the status of every single order, and ensured my company did not lose major contracts. Why could I not simply state that? How in the world was this bragging when it was simply the T R U T H? My mindset was not serving me, and I knew it. But how could I overcome these feelings? These feelings were paralyzing my career, and I desperately needed a way out, a plan, a new mindset.

So What?!

Two years later, I was promoted again. Not because I completely overcame these feelings, but because my former manager, who I reported to prior to my first promotion, spoke so highly of my potential to the hiring manager. After a grueling panel interview with who would become my peers, I was promoted again. For the next several years, I continued to struggle with stating my value, and to make matters worse, the company changed the cadence to have accomplishment sessions twice per year.

While my team and I were doing great and exceeding targets, I needed to step up as the rookie. Thankfully, the new director took me under her wing. She continued to challenge me in this area, and I finally reached a point where I could at least state what my team had done that year. I would say things like, "We met the key performance metrics," or "We completed the annual project."

The following year, we were met with an announcement that our current director was leaving to go to another part of the organization, and a new woman was replacing her. The entire team was in shock. I was particularly worried because I was losing a mentor that I had direct access to any time I needed. To make matters worse, we were right at the end of the year, and it was time to submit our annual accomplishments. I was worried but not as much as usual since I had mastered writing down the checklist of things my team had done.

Typically, the team would submit this information electronically within a software application, but this new director asked for us all to print them out and set up a meeting with her to go over them. I remember walking into her office so proud of my two-page list of accomplishments. I sat there in silence as she read them, and it seemed like it took her forever. When she had finally finished reading every single word, she grabbed a red marker pen and wrote in very large letters at a diagonal (as if she was voiding a check), "SO WHAT?" She then handed my pages back to me, looked me straight in the face, and said, "If you can't explain to me why these things are important, they mean nothing. If you cannot answer the question, 'SO WHAT?' for everything you have listed here, you need to delete it. Now go back and redo this."

I was in complete shock and disbelief, which was quickly followed by anger (which I now know was driven by my fear). How dare she write all over my document and challenge me that way? In one stroke of the pen, she dismantled what took me hours to complete. And now, I have to go back to the drawing board and answer the question, "SO WHAT?" This woman has lost her mind. I managed to keep my face straight. I took the document back and returned to my office.

Looking back at this moment, I realized that she was one of the people planted in my career to be my sandpaper, to make me smoother, to make me more polished. While the sanding process is messy and hurts a bit, in the end, the wood is beautiful, poised, and ready to serve.

When I got back to my office, I was frustrated and overwhelmed. I kept staring at my paper with the red pen markup as if it was bleeding and in need of a bandage. But then something beautiful happened. I had to admit that what she said really made sense. I decided to be more coachable, to allow her to push me beyond where I was at. In order to change, you have to surrender and be willing to go through the process. Resisting would not have served me at all. I had to say to myself, "I will not allow my career to be governed by my feelings!"

I sat down and looked over my accomplishments one by one and asked myself, "SO WHAT?" If I could not answer that question, I removed the accomplishment because there was no point in including it if I could not articulate its value to the business. After about an hour, I had a huge smile on my face because I knew that I was getting to that place they call "from good to great" in this area. I was immediately thankful for her candid feedback and happy that I embraced the not so gentle nudge that she gave me. I walked back to her office with the expectation that her red pen would not find its way bleeding all over my document this time – and it didn't.

PART TWO

The Business of Self Promotion

Address Your BS and Inspect Your Foundation

Before you can get into the business of self-promoting without feeling like you're bragging, you must first address why you feel that way. I shared my story about my upbringing, which planted the seeds of me believing I needed permission to speak up for myself. You need to do the same self-evaluation, or nothing I recommend beyond this point will help. You need to inspect your B.S., which is your Belief System. Take a good look at where you are right now in your career and how your beliefs have contributed to that success or demise. What do you believe about yourself, your career, your capabilities? Which of these beliefs support your career goals? Are these beliefs limiting you or enabling you? If you're struggling to answer these questions, I recommend applying the G.O.A.L. method to your inspection. **Get Out And L**ook.

Remove your personal feelings and tendency to block the truth, get outside of the situation and address it head-on as if you were giving someone else advice. If you take yourself out of the situation, I guarantee you'll be able to easily rattle off the belief areas that are limiting your career.

Once you've identified these areas, spend time inspecting your foundation by asking yourself where these limiting beliefs came from.

Was there a moment in your career, or were you like me -- taught these things growing up but misapplied them? You've reached the proverbial fork in the road where it is time to decide to tear down that old foundation and build a new one.

Wise HAT Detox

TEARING DOWN THE OLD FOUNDATION

After years of struggling in my career with bad Habits, horrible influence from the wrong Associations ("friends"/coworkers), and toxic Thoughts about all of it, I saw how it was also affecting my relationships and, believe it or not, my health!

Finally, I realized that my career choices were not serving me, and I had to make some difficult decisions. I had to change my HAT. They say that knowledge is power; however, knowing something and doing something are two totally different things. This is the main thing that holds us back. We are full of knowledge but fail to actually apply that knowledge to our careers. For me, it took my company almost firing me before I realized that I was giving them the keys to my career, to do with it what they pleased.

We often like to blame others for what's not going right in our careers, but we have to take a step back and identify the areas where we've given away the keys. Which of you would leave the keys to your home or your car in the outside keyhole for everyone to see? If you did that, would it make sense to blame the thief that took your car or entered your home? Oh, I know, you're thinking, "Jae, any decent good Samaritan would not enter my home or steal my car even if I left the keys out." While that may be true, have you heard of crimes of opportunity? Now, I'm in no way advocating for or defending thieves but what I am saying is, we have to stop and take ownership of our issues and eliminate the opportunities that we give to others to determine our career destination goals. If your goal is to advance in your career, ask yourself:

1. Do I have the right foundation in place to accomplish this goal?
2. What are my daily Habits, Associations, and Thoughts like?
3. Am I late to work and/or meetings on a regular basis?
4. Is my work flawed and often in need of correction/adjustments because I'm multitasking, or do I have too much on my plate to truly focus?
5. Am I coachable, or am I the person that no one can correct at all?
6. Is my character and my reputation in alignment?
7. Am I aligned with the right people?
8. Am I chronically over-functioning?
9. Am I so afraid of failure that I'm paralyzed?
10. Do I hang out with folks that are committed to comfort?

It is time for you to stop being the woman that has things happen to her and start being the woman that makes things happen!

These were the questions that I asked myself and had to face the beautiful truth about (I don't like to say the ugly truth because the truth will make you free, and that is a beautiful thing!). Over time, I began to make adjustments in these three areas in my career and began to see that practical wisdom was helping me make real changes. I created the WiseHAT Detox Guide to help you identify the top three toxic Habits, Associations, and Thoughts that are interrupting your journey to success in your career.

We only focus on the top three because this is the second reason why we struggle because we get overwhelmed with the process.

When you look at all the areas you need and want to change, it can be overwhelming. But just as you did not get this way overnight, you likely won't change it overnight as well. This is a process that takes time. I realize we live in a world where everything looks instant, but I promise you, it's all an illusion.

The WiseHAT Detox Guide is designed to help you start on your journey to rid yourself of unwise and unhealthy Habits, Associations, and Thoughts and replace them with wise and healthy ones. You're going to identify the top three bad Habits, Associations, and Thoughts impacting your career that you want to get rid of while also identifying the top three that you want to maintain or produce.

Throughout this guide, keep your mind focused on what you want to change. Don't allow yourself to get distracted with the 'how.' We will address that later.

Habits

WHAT ARE YOU DOING?

I have a Public Service Announcement; it does not take 21 days to form a new habit! So, where did that come from? Blame it on an old-fashioned game of telephone. This all started when a plastic surgeon named Maxwell Maltz observed and wrote in his research that it took his patients 21 days to get used to their new faces. Over time, and just like the telephone game, that observation became the saying , "It takes 21 days to form a new habit." The truth is, more research has been done that indicates forming a new habit may take you much longer than 21 days, depending on the habit and the situation. In reality, the average time it takes to form a new habit is 66 days. (James Clear, 2020 – Retrieved July 2020 from https://jamesclear.com/new-habit)

Now, take a deep, cleansing breath in and out. You've likely been doing these Habits for years, so let's remove the false expectations that you will rid yourself of the old ones and have brand new ones after 21 days. Repeat after me, "this is a journey, and I will make progress one day at a time!" With each step, the good news is that you will get closer to shifting your behavior and actually forming new Habits!

Habits are formed of three things: 1) the trigger, 2) the routine, and 3) the reward. When evaluating your Habits, ask yourself, what has prompted me to do this behavior (the trigger), what is the actual habit (the routine), and what is the perceived benefit or outcome as a result of doing this (the reward)? (James Clear, 2020 – Retrieved July 2020 from https://habitsacademy.com) For example, one of my bad Habits used to be multitasking while on conference calls. I would be on a conference call or in a meeting and get a phone or email alert (the trigger), and I would stop focusing on the meeting/call and look at my phone or computer to read the email or alert (routine). I was in fear that I would miss something if I did not read the alerts immediately, so I thought multitasking would allow me to stay abreast of everything (the reward).

In reality, I was cheating myself from the present and missing something taking place in that meeting that required my attention. This then generated another bad Habit, calling or asking my peer what I missed in the very same meeting that we were both in together and I was supposed to be paying attention to. Asking "what did I miss" one time too many will impact your reputation because now you will be labeled as the person who is distracted and not productive in meetings.

∼

Use the worksheet below to identify your top three Habits that you want to eliminate, maintain, and produce. You can also download this worksheet at www.wisehatconsultingcontent.com.

Now Let's Get to Work!

Use the table below to identify your top 3 Habits that you want to eliminate, maintain and produce.

Things to consider: How long have I been doing this Habit? Do I want to change it? What do I want to replace it with?

List below the top 3 Habits you want to eliminate	List below the top 3 Habits you want to maintain	List below the top 3 Habits you want to produce

Associations

❦❧

EVALUATE YOUR ENVIRONMENT

"You are the average of the 5 people you spend the most time with."

— *JIM ROHN*

The key is, you cannot change the people around you, but you can change the people around you. It is all about geography (read that again).

I remember very early on in my career having to make an Association change. I worked in a massive call center in the late '90s and sat on the "party row." If you've ever worked in a call center, you know all about the party rows. We were the loudest row, barely taking any calls, always late to work, and often arguing with customers on the phone. I was the one that was chronically late and not by long. Again, if you've ever worked in a call center, you know that one minute is considered late.

Due to the horrendous Bay Area traffic, I had a two-hour drive to and from work. I would leave my home at 7 a.m. to make it to work by 9 a.m. I found myself arriving at least twice per week between 9:01 and 9:05 a.m. There's a saying out there about arriving on time. "If you're on time, you're late, and if you're 15 (some say 10) minutes early, you're on time." Unbeknownst to me, too many of these late occurrences got me on the radar of my management team.

I had no clue they were about to discipline me for my tardiness and that I actually had enough of them to be terminated outright. Ironically (but not really), around that time, I was also having a moment with myself as well. I looked at my surroundings and knew I was associated with the wrong crowd. I wanted so much more for my career, and I knew I was destined far beyond that call center, so I had to make some difficult choices. While I really liked my coworkers and truly enjoyed laughing and joking around with them, the truth is, I was not there for the laughs and jokes. I had a job to do and could not afford to lose my job. At the time, I shared an apartment with my sister and had just bought a new car. There was no opportunity to run back home to my parents.

One night after prayer, I asked God for wisdom on what to do, and He gave me this scripture: "Wherefore come out from among them, and be ye separate, saith the Lord, and touch not the unclean thing, and I will receive you" (II Corinthians 6:17, KJV). "Come out from among them" needed no interpretation. It was very clear I needed to change my Associations. I decided right then to write a letter to my management team explaining the epiphany I had regarding my career, how I realized that I was allowing the behaviors of others to impact my actions (wrong Associations) and requested that I change my seat.

I walked into work the next morning and asked to meet with my manager. I presented him with the letter, and I could tell at that moment that I'd taken the wind out of his sails somewhat. I recall him saying he'd plan to meet with me soon about my attendance issue, but he was glad that I'd come to him first. He then asked where I wanted to sit and if I'd also wanted to change my hours to accommodate my tardiness issue. I'd already given thought to where I wanted to sit. I had picked the row with the folks who took the most calls and always won contests and worked on special projects for the center.

As for my start time, I told him I wanted to keep my original start time, and I would be sure to never be tardy again. He reluctantly agreed to that and told me to move my things at the end of my shift. This was the hard part -- going back to my desk and packing my things. Seeing the faces of my coworkers as I packed and telling them that I asked to move to another row and seeing the bewildered look on their faces that quickly turned to "Oh, she thinks she's better than us" stares. I knew I was doing the right thing, and I could not allow peer pressure to trick me out of my job.

Many years later, I learned two things: 1) They were about to fire me for my tardiness. Had I not come to them, I would have been fired. 2) The "leader" of that row, who ended up being my very good friend later, wrote me a letter months after I moved and told me that she understood why I moved, and she was not upset with me for that. She knew that it was the right thing for me to do.

This is why you cannot be concerned with how people feel when you establish healthy boundaries. You cannot let their feelings stop you. Not that you need to be rude, but you must choose yourself first! As for my tardiness, I started leaving my home at 5 a.m. just to avoid the traffic. I would arrive to work by 5:45 a.m. and sleep in the parking lot until 8:55 a.m. (3 hours and 10 minutes) so that I'd never be late again! Sometimes, it takes a radical action to beget a radical change.

There's a scripture in the Bible that says bad company corrupts good character (I Corinthians 15:33, NIV). It wasn't that I was around bad people, but their company was bad, meaning the way in which they chose to conduct themselves was not in alignment with the goals I had for myself and my career. Alignment is all about getting in a line that is meant for you! Associations are vital everywhere in your life and especially in the workplace. Had I not made those adjustments, I would have eventually been fired and unable to continue in the 20+ year career that I have now.

It is important to note that changing your Associations is not just about people but also about how you associate things. For example, if you associate your career or self-promotion with pain and frustration, you need to change those Associations as well.

Ladies, this is the part where you decide to truly identify what Associations are not serving your career and what adjustments you need to make. This can be accomplished by assessing the energy produced by these Associations. The ones that drain your energy may need to be eliminated or modified. It is also very important to do a real self-assessment and understand if your energy is being drained because of YOU. Is there something you're doing that could preserve your energy? Sometimes we participate in the performance with an invisible script. So, if you're the type of person who is not keenly self-aware, I challenge you to find someone you trust, capable of telling you the "beautiful truth" to help you answer this question.

～

Use the worksheet below to identify the Associations you want to eliminate, maintain, and produce.

EVALUATE YOUR ENVIRONMENT

Use the table below to identify your top 3 Associations that you want to eliminate, maintain and produce.

Things to consider: How long have I had this Association/relationship? Is it draining my energy? Am I the reason my energy is being drained?

List below the top 3 Associations you want to eliminate	List below the top 3 Associations you want to maintain	List below the top 3 Associations you want to produce

Thoughts

E xperts say that the average person has about 12,000 to 60,000 thoughts per day. Of those thousands of thoughts, approximately 80% were negative, and 95% were the same repetitive thoughts as the day before. Every time we have a thought, our brain releases chemicals. A negative thought draws away from the energy your brain needs to perform at its normal capacity. (TLEX Institute, Retrieved July 2020 from https://tlexinstitute.com/how-to-effectively-have-more-positive-thoughts/)

Your Thoughts are vital to your ability to make any changes in your career, including your Habits and Associations. If you do not address your Thoughts, you may never see the changes in your career that you spend so much time daydreaming about. What do you think of yourself, of others, and your capabilities? It's not who you are that's holding you back; it's who you think you're not!

Thoughts are like ants. When ants are looking for food, they send out a scout ant. When it finds food, it marks a scent path and returns to the colony to let them know that it has found a place of potential, a place blooming with food! Before you know it, there are hundreds of ants invading that area. So, in the same way, one negative thought may pop into your mind, and if you don't address it, your mind is flooded with negative Thoughts that are coming fast and furious; these are ANTS - AUTOMATIC NEGATIVE THOUGHTS!

I challenge you to spend one day thinking about what you're thinking about. Try to jot down the random Thoughts you have (hint, you won't be able to capture all of them), and see if they are negative, positive, repetitive, or outlandish. If your mind is filled with negative Thoughts, it's no surprise that you are tired by the end of the day. The chemicals released in your brain that have been produced by that negative thought are actually draining your energy. Some of us are exhausted not because we don't get enough sleep but because our Thoughts are so negative, our brains cannot keep up. It's time to kill the ANTS associated with your career. Some of us need a thought transplant!

～

Use the worksheet below to identify the Thoughts you want to eliminate, maintain, and produce.

Let's Kill the A.N.T.'s!

Use the table below to identify your top 3 Thoughts that you want to eliminate, maintain and produce.

Things to consider: What are the negative Thoughts that I rehearse in my mind over and over again? Are these positive or negative Thoughts ? Do I truly believe these Thoughts?

List below the top 3 Thoughts you want to eliminate	List below the top 3 Thoughts you want to maintain	List below the top 3 Thoughts you want to produce

Now What?

Detoxing is about ridding yourself of toxins. In this case, toxic Habits, Associations, and Thoughts (HAT's). Shift your focus to the detox and not how long it will take you to complete it. This is about true and lasting life changes. It's time to shift your mindset away from a fixed mind focused on "quick fixes" to a growth mindset that focuses on what you already have available to you to achieve the success you desire.

Focus on the Top 3 HATs You Want to Eliminate

For each HAT, come up with at least 3 different ways of how you will begin to address them. How do you do that? By asking yourself, what does a person who does not have this bad Habit, Association, or Thought do? For example, if one of your Habits is oversleeping, ask yourself, what does a person who doesn't oversleep do? Perhaps they get more disciplined and go to bed earlier or move their alarm clock across the room.

Now commit to the process and execute! Remember those 21 days I mentioned earlier? Here's where those days actually make sense!

Wise HAT 21 Day Detox Execution Plan

BUILD A NEW FOUNDATION

Now that you have the things you want to eliminate and a plan of action, take one area at a time (Habits, Associations & Thoughts), and focus on that area for 7 days with your plan to execute. There are 3 areas you are addressing for a total of 21 days of detoxing! Each day review your plan for the HAT you focused on.

Just like with any detox, once you rid yourself of toxins, you must replenish with the right things.

In order to form a new Habit, you need to consider these three things: 1) Is it appealing (do you want to do it)? 2) Is it achievable (can you actually do this behavior)? and 3) Is it activated (what prompt or trigger will you create or already exists to do this behavior)? (James Clear, 2020 -Retrieved July 2020 from https://habitsacademy.com) Keep in mind that you may have to spend some time assessing and changing your Associations and Thoughts to answer these questions effectively.

Right now, you may be thinking that the Habits you know you need are not appealing, achievable, or activated. If they don't seem appealing to you, it may be a matter of will versus skill. If they are not achievable, you may need to scale it back a bit because sometimes we want instant change to things we've been doing for years, and it really does not work that way. Besides, going too big too soon when it comes to changing Habits will likely set you up for failure and have you repeating the same vicious cycle where you never see change.

WiseHAT Tips on Building a New Foundation:

> Motivation often comes after you start a behavior, not before.
> If you slip up one time, don't lose heart – no room for perfectionism.
> Shift your focus to starting the Habit and not how long it will take you to form the new Habit.
> I recommend downloading the worksheets and adding them to a vision board or a place that you'll see them daily. A visual trigger will remind you of what you truly want!

PART THREE

Have A System

Humbitious Woman Foundation

⚬⚬⚬

"If you fail to plan, you plan to fail."

N ow that you've taken the time to build a new foundation by changing your HAT, you must have a plan to execute self-promotion with ease. You're going to do that by investing time instead of wasting time.

Let's start by creating a "fact sheet" that you will use to house all of your accomplishments as they occur. This fact sheet is basically a document capturing all the wonderful contributions you've made to your company. Remember, you are not bragging; you are stating the facts of what you and/or your team accomplished.

I typically fill my fact sheet with enough info and data points to recall what was accomplished, who was involved, and what the impact was on the business. Many will start with creating the document but fail to invest the time to update the document on a regular basis because they are "too busy." In order to effectively execute this, you need to prioritize by proactively carving out time for you to reflect on what you've accomplished recently. The cadence of how often you do this will be determined by how often you need to provide your accomplishments within your company and your memory span. For example, your company may require accomplishments only twice per year; however, if your memory span is short, so you might want to consider carving out time every 30 days.

The second key to this is being consistent by not allowing something or someone to steal that time. You must treat this like a regular meeting that you have with the most important person in your career -- you! Having said that, be wise about the time you select. Whatever days of the week and times of the day your workload is the lightest will be the most beneficial and will further allow you to stick to the schedule.

Now go to your calendar and block off the time. Go ahead, create that meeting! Label it "not available, working on accomplishments" or "reviewing monthly accomplishments." The duration of the meeting will be determined by how often you will do this. For example, you may set it up once per month for one hour or bi-weekly for 30 minutes. When that meeting comes up, resist the urge to skip over it and do other things because you are busy. Remember, in order to see returns, you must invest. You are investing a small portion of your time in comparison to the rest of your month, but your return will be well worth it! This proactive investment of your time will bring great peace and minimal effort when the time comes for you to provide your accomplishments to your company. When that time does come, you will simply select the appropriate items from your fact sheet, polish the verbiage and data points up a bit so that it reads well, and provide it on whatever tool your company utilizes to submit accomplishments. It's that simple!

How to Write Effective Accomplishments

‹❦›

Now that you have a plan in place with an established cadence for when you will invest the time to proactively capture your accomplishments, you need to be clear on what is important and what isn't to your Company. In other words, in order to write effective accomplishments, you must first understand what is expected of you. What is valued by your company and your specific business unit or sector? What are your specific goals? What core competencies does your business unit expect you to possess? What are the company and business unit goals for the year?

Your accomplishments must align with whatever these goals and competencies are. Otherwise, they are meaningless. I'll let you in on a little secret. This is how you answer the question, "SO WHAT?" for every accomplishment you list. Utilize your company goals and expectations by aligning your goals to them. For example, if your company has a goal of reducing the cycle time or churn on a specific product or process by 50% and your work has yielded a 55% reduction, after describing your accomplishment, utilize that already stated and established company goal to describe why this accomplishment was important to the business and how it added value, how you added value. This will clearly remind them why they hired you and your value to your company and your team.

Now tell me, does any of this sound like you're bragging? I beg to differ. This is simply you reporting the data, the results, the outcome of the things you worked so hard on throughout the year. Getting good at doing this does not make you arrogant. It makes you acute, adept, resourceful, agile, effective, bright – all the words you want to see and hear when receiving feedback from your leadership. *(Check out additional tips on writing effective accomplishments in the resources chapter.)*

Traits of a Humbitious Woman in the Workplace

If you're going to be an Humbitious Woman®, you are going to have to change your HAT and become comfortable with being uncomfortable, keenly self-aware, coachable at all times, talking about yourself, speaking up in meetings, a woman who knows and communicates her personal brand, willing to volunteer for projects/initiatives outside of her comfort zone, vocal and unapologetic about her ambitions, and most importantly always willing to serve.

With all of this, you must have established healthy boundaries that support your HAT. Just because you are willing to serve does not mean that you must serve everyone and everything. It's important to teach others how you want to be treated in the workplace by establishing healthy boundaries. This means that you can't be the go-to person for everything, and you must learn how to manage your day effectively. I don't subscribe to the saying that there is a "work/life balance" because you only have one life, and things will never be completely balanced.

Balance implies that you must take away from one thing to give to the other. However, harmony between your work and your life is what should be sought. Harmony shows relations and differences amongst things while allowing them to work in agreement with one another. Imagine an orchestra in harmony and the beautiful sound that comes when each instrument is making its own unique sound while it supports the similarities and differences of the other instruments in order to produce the song.

A humbitious woman prioritizes, slows down to ensure the quality of her work aligns with her brand, stays focused, and learns to delegate wherever possible. How is this accomplished? By addressing the W.I.N. – **WHAT'S IMPORTANT NOW**. Focusing on the WIN is like juggling a set of balls, some made of glass and some made of rubber. What happens when a glass ball is dropped? It crashes and makes a lot of noise and will draw lots of attention to you.

Conversely, when the rubber ball is dropped, it makes a dull thud which can barely be heard. In fact, the ball bounces right back up to you! In the same way, the WIN's of the day are your glass balls that must be addressed, or they will make a loud crash and perhaps generate a phone call from your manager or peer who is expecting you to make a deadline. Everything else can wait until after the WIN's are addressed. Be prepared to be challenged in this area because everyone thinks their issue is urgent, but not everything is an emergency.

Overcome the Fear of Others

None of what I've shared in this book can be accomplished if you fear what other people think. It took me a long time to realize that my uniqueness is what made me special. It was my "secret sauce," my brand, my trademark, and the moment I learned and started to embrace it, I was able to overcome the fear of others. To be clear, I'm not suggesting that you show up to work tomorrow, telling everyone what's on your mind and giving them a piece of it. Nor do I want you to hide your rudeness or lack of professionalism behind being your "authentic self" (if the shoe fits). What I mean by overcoming fear is that you do not allow fear to keep you from being humbitious. I remember the moment I realized this with certainty.

Fifteen years into my career, I was at the top of my game. I managed a team of 35 engineers and project managers working on cutting-edge technology. I was esteemed by my peers and leadership, I had the highest appraisal rating and glowing feedback, but I was miserable. Why? Because I had a strong desire to go to another part of the company. I was in the engineering sector and wanted badly to go to HR. At the time, it was unheard of to want to make such a drastic change, and I was so afraid to share this with my leadership. I'd made up in my mind that they would think I was not happy because I wanted to take my talents to another part of the company and change their mind about my performance because of it, so I kept my mouth shut. What I had to realize is that my career is just that, mine.

While I need support, mentorship, and the right alignment to be successful, my desires for my career should not be overshadowed by what someone else thought I should be doing. After a year or so, I finally got up the nerve to share my career goals with them. I told them I wanted to go to HR because my passion was helping others become better versions of themselves. While I could do that somewhat as a leader managing 35 people, our primary focus was on our technology deliverables.

I knew I could make a greater impact by training others and focusing on the actual business of people. I was already serving in this capacity every chance I got by hosting webinars within the company's employee resource groups, but that was not enough for me. To my surprise, they were all so very supportive of my goals. One of them even introduced me to key leaders in HR who were willing to sit down with me and give advice on the next steps. That experience taught me that FEAR truly is FALSE EVIDENCE APPEARING REAL, and I would no longer allow fear to keep me from being humbitious.

~

What are you afraid to do in your career because you're concerned about what others will think?

I challenge you to take a step and overcome the fear, but before you do, make sure you've changed your HAT, and you take your next steps HUMBITIOUSLY!

Humbitious Woman Resources

If what I've shared in this book resonates with you and you want to dig deeper into how to change your HAT, find your voice, take back control of your career, overcome the fear of others, and start to see your career goals come into fruition; the **Humbitious Woman®** **Academy** is for you! The academy is a 90-day online program designed to help women take back control of their careers. Visit my website to find out more www.wisehatconsulting.com.

Do's and Don'ts of Writing Effective Accomplishments

When writing your accomplishments, you must have some practical things in addition to what I shared in the How to Write Effective Accomplishments Section. Check out my Do's and Don'ts list below.

Do

- Utilize bullet formatting when documenting
- Be able to quantify your work or assign a quantifiable data point to your accomplishment
- CHECK SPELLING!

Do Not

- Speak in first or third person but rather start with actionable verbs such as *conducted*, *led*, *maintained*, etc.
- Believe that you are not a leader, so accomplishments are not important. Whether you lead people directly or not, your accomplishments matter!

Practice: *Revise the accomplishments below to be more effective.*

Ineffective Accomplishment	Effective Accomplishment
I worked on projects with peers.	
I completed 10 work orders.	
I always have a positive attitude about sharing knowledge and experience with my peers.	
Attended team meetings and calls.	
My worksheets are maintained consistently throughout each day.	
Met goal.	

About the Author

Jocquice "Jae" Spikes is a 24+ year corporate leader, serving in various engineering, training, and HR sectors. She is passionate about helping women become better versions of themselves. Jocquice has created and facilitated many webinars and workshops specializing in bridging the gap between technical aptitude and professional development for thousands of corporate employees. Jocquice has a Bachelor of Science in Organizational Management from Patten University and an MBA from Golden Gate University. She is the recipient of the Career Communications Women of Color STEM Association Technology Rising Star Award for her outstanding professional achievement and the President's Volunteer Service Award for her dedication to community service.

Her mission and purpose are to harness decades of experience and share these tangible tips and tools with other women. As the founder of WiseHAT® Consulting, a career consulting company that empowers corporate women who feel stuck and burned out in their careers change their HAT (Habits, Associations, and Thoughts) to take back control of their careers, Jocquice's passion for helping women be bold to excel in their careers is realized. Her signature programs include the Humbitious Woman® Academy, Humbitious Woman® Podcast, and the WiseHAT® Detox Guide. Jocquice loves to show and teach women the practical but very effective ways to navigate their career successfully." As a leader, she believes leadership is all about servanthood.

For more information about Jocquice schedule a 30-minute consultation. Visit her website at www.wisehatconsulting.com.